AVERROES

SCHOLAR OF CLASSICAL AND ISLAMIC PHILOSOPHY

PHYSICIANS, SCIENTISTS, AND MATHEMATICIANS OF THE ISLAMIC WORLD™

AVERROES

SCHOLAR OF CLASSICAL AND ISLAMIC PHILOSOPHY

BRIDGET LIM
AND LIZ SONNEBORN

ROSEN PUBLISHING®
New York

Published in 2017 by The Rosen Publishing Group, Inc.
29 East 21st Street, New York, NY 10010

First Edition

Library of Congress Cataloging-in-Publication Data

Names: Lim, Bridget, author.
Title: Averroes (Ibn Rushd) : Scholar of Classical and Islamic Philosophy / Bridget Lim and Liz Sonneborn.
Description: First Edition. | New York : Rosen Publishing, 2017. | Series: Physicians, scientists, and mathematicians of the Islamic world | Includes bibliographical references and index.
Identifiers: LCCN 2015047628 | ISBN 9781508171416 (library bound)
Subjects: LCSH: Averroèes, 1126-1198.
Classification: LCC B749.Z7 L56 2016 | DDC 181/.92--dc23
LC record available at http://lccn.loc.gov/2015047628

Unless otherwise attributed, all quoted material comes from *Averroes: His Life, Works and Influence* by Majid Fakhry.

CONTENTS

INTRODUCTION

During the Middle Ages, the Arab world was experiencing a remarkable burst of scholarship and scientific advancement. Thanks to their understanding of the importance of cultural and intellectual pursuits, the caliphs who ruled the region were known to assemble courts. On these courts sat the most intelligent scholars of the Islamic world. These men studied the works of ancient Greek philosophers—works that had been all but cast aside in Europe by this time. The Muslim scholars studied the ancient Greeks, interpreting their philosophies through their own Islamic culture and faith, and made significant advancements of their own.

The man we call Averroes was one of the great thinkers of the Muslim world during the Middle Ages. He studied the philosophy of ancient Greeks like Plato and Aristotle and wrote brilliant commentary about them. He also was an accomplished physician and judge.

As the story goes, one day in 1169, Averroes arrived for an important meeting in the beautiful city of Marrakesh, in northern Africa. Averroes is his Latin name, used in the west; his true name was Abu al-Walid ibn Rushd. Then in his early forties, Averroes lived a comfortable and quiet life in Córdoba, a city in the north of al-Andalus,

Abu al-Walid ibn Rushd is known in the West by his Latin name, Averroes. His scholarship on Artistotelian philosophy gained him renown in the Muslim world and also in Europe.

which is in Andalusia of present-day Spain. There, he studied and wrote about law and medicine.

Averroes was invited to meet with Abu Yaqub Yusuf. The year before, Yusuf had become the second caliph, or ruler, of the Almohad dynasty. At that time the Almohads controlled a large empire including what is now northern Africa and southern Spain.

When Averroes arrived, he saw that the caliph already had another guest, Averroes's old friend and teacher Abu Bakr ibn Tufayl. Like Averroes, Ibn Tufayl was a scholar. In addition to being a physician, he studied the works of Muslim philosophers. Ibn Tufayl was particularly interested in the works of Abu Ali al-Husayn ibn Sina, also known as Avicenna (980–1037). Avicenna was an expert in the works of Aristotle, a philosopher who lived in ancient Greece some 1,400 years earlier.

As the meeting began, Averroes had no idea what to expect from the caliph. But soon, he became very nervous. According to Majid Fakhry's *Averroes: His Life, Works and Influence* (2001), the caliph immediately began asking Averroes some extremely disturbing questions: "What do the philosophers believe regarding heaven? Is it eternal or created in time?"

Such questions were hardly new. Long ago, the ancient Greek philosophers had developed their own answers. Plato had argued that the world had a definite beginning, while Aristotle maintained it had always existed. Many Muslim scholars, however, vehemently denounced both philosophers' arguments about the beginnings of the universe. In these scholars' eyes, the ideas advanced by the Greeks directly contradicted the Quran (the holy scripture of Islam) in many ways—from their views on the origin of the world to their ideas about the existence of an afterlife. Muslims believed that the Quran was the word of God, delivered to humankind by the prophet Muhammad. To contradict the Quran was therefore an offense against God.

Understandably, Averroes was leery of Yusuf's questions. Was the caliph trying to trap him into saying something inappropriate? What would Yusuf do if Averroes said something he did not agree with?

Averroes decided to play it safe. As recounted by Oliver Leaman in *Averroes and His Philosophy* (1998), Averroes developed a strategy: "I began to make excuses and deny that I had ever concerned myself with philosophic learning; for I did not know what Ibn Tufayl had told him on the subject."

The caliph saw Averroes's discomfort and tried to set his mind at ease. He explained at length his own understanding of the views of Greek philosophers as well as the charges against them leveled by great Muslim thinkers. As a young man, Yusuf had spent some time in the city of Seville in al-Andalus. There, he socialized with the philosophers, scholars, and poets, absorbing their knowledge and developing an appetite for more. Through his own studies, the caliph had become something of an expert on both Greek and Muslim philosophers. Averroes was quite impressed. He later told a friend that he found in Yusuf "a profuseness of learning I did not suspect in a specialist in that field."

Convinced the prince wanted an open discussion, Averroes began to expound his own studies in philosophy. The prince was excited by his expertise. According to Leaman in *Averroes and His Philosophy*, Averroes later recalled that the get-together ended on a happy note: "Thus he continued to set me at ease until I spoke, and he learned what was my competence in that subject; and when I withdrew he ordered for me a gift of money, a magnificent robe of honor and a steed!"

The caliph had good reason to be pleased. Before the meeting, Yusuf had been struggling in his quest to master Greek philosophy. He was particularly puzzled by many of Aristotle's texts, which he read in Arabic translations from the original Greek. The prince had asked Ibn Tufayl to write commentaries on Aristotle to help him interpret the Greek philosopher's meaning.

Ibn Tufayl had declined, saying he was too old to take on such a difficult project. He instead recommended Averroes for the job.

Ibn Tufayl then set about convincing Averroes of the project's worth. As recorded by Leaman, Ibn Tufayl explained, "If someone would tackle these books, summarize them and expound their aims, after understanding them thoroughly, it would be easier for people to grasp them…I expect you will be equal to it, from what I know of the excellence of your mind, the purity of your nature, and the intensity of your application to science."

To the caliph's delight, Averroes agreed to devote himself to the study of Aristotle. The decision changed the course of his life. For years to come, he wrote comprehensive commentaries on the great Greek philosopher, ranging from short paraphrases of Aristotle's words to lengthy, line-by-line analyses approachable by only the most learned scholars.

Averroes's decision also changed the course of world culture. In time, his commentaries reintroduced Europe to the breadth of Greek philosophy. As one of the greatest interpreters of Aristotle, Averroes and his work forged a crucial link between ancient and modern thought.

CHAPTER ONE

THE DEVELOPMENT OF THE ISLAMIC WORLD

Averroes was born in 1126 in Córdoba, a city of wealth and wisdom that fostered his emergence as one of the greatest thinkers of his time. At this time Córdoba was the capital of al-Andalus (as Muslim Spain was called). As great as the city was during Averroes's time, it had an even more illustrious past as perhaps the world's most cosmopolitan city. According to María Rosa Menocal, about 150 years earlier, in the tenth century, the German nun Hrosvitha described Córdoba as "the brilliant ornament of the world … wealthy and famous and known for its pleasures and resplendent in all things."

THE PROPHET MUHAMMAD AND THE QURAN

The story of Averroes's Córdoba is rooted in a far-away place and time—the Arabian Peninsula during the sixth century. At that time, Arabia was not unified,

According to the Quran, the archangel Gabriel visited Muhammad and served as the messenger for the Prophet's first revelation from God. Muhammad began preaching these revelations, thus founding the religion of Islam.

neither politically or religiously. Its population included Christians and Jews, as well as people who believed in local cults that worshipped natural forces and objects as deities. There were some urban centers in Arabia, but many areas were covered by deserts, and therefore could not support large populations. The people of the deserts were largely nomads. Many were members of tribes led by hereditary leaders.

In the town of Mecca in western Arabia, Muhammad ibn Abd Allah ibn Hashim was born in about 570. He belonged to the Quraysh tribe that then controlled Mecca. The Quraysh oversaw a shrine there, associated with the cult of the moon god Hubal.

In about 610, Muhammad began seeing visions and hearing voices. At first frightened, he came to believe these messages were from God. He compiled these revelations into a book called the Quran (also spelled Koran). The Quran is the sacred scripture of Islam, which, along with Judaism and Christianity, is one of the three great monotheistic religions in the world today. Islam's followers, known as Muslims, hold that the Quran is the literal word of God.

The Quran calls on Muslims to worship only one God. It also requires them to pray regularly and obey set rules of behavior during their life on earth. Muslims believe that they can achieve salvation and be sent to heaven after death only by obeying these rules.

Muhammad began preaching his message in about 613. Devoted to the worship of a single God, his words posed a direct challenge to the beliefs of the Quraysh and other tribes. Even so, he found some followers in Mecca and other nearby towns, including Yathrib. The people of Yathrib invited Muhammad to move there and essentially become its ruler. He made the journey from Mecca to Yathrib in 622. This event was called the *hijra* (meaning "emigration"). Yathrib itself was renamed Medina, or "city of the Prophet."

THE EMERGENCE OF AN ISLAMIC EMPIRE

After the hijra, Muhammad became a political as well as a religious leader. Under the Prophet's leadership, Medina struggled with Mecca to win the support of other towns and tribal groups. Muhammad's religious message attracted many groups to his side. When he died in 632, he held western Arabia under his sway.

Following the Prophet's death, leadership of his followers fell to a line of caliphs (caliph literally means "successor to the prophet"). The first was Abu Bakr al-Asamm, Muhammad's father-in-law. Through military campaigns, he brought all of Arabia into an emerging Islamic empire. Under Abu Bakr and his successor, Umar ibn al-Kattab, Islam's influence continued to spread—to the west into the Byzantine Empire and to the east into the Sassanid (Persian) Empire. Many of the people in these regions were neither Arab nor Muslim. Therefore, although the Islamic Empire was guided by the laws of the Quran, its popultion included people of many different ethnicities and religions.

Islam faced a crisis in 656 when the third caliph, Uthman ibn Affan, was murdered. He was suceeded by Ali ibn Abi Talib. But some people, including members of the Umayyad clan, who were related to Uthman, opposed Ali's rule. The two sides almost went to battle, before Ali was assassinated in 661. Eager for the infighting to end, a majority of Muslims decided to follow Muawiyah ibn Abi Sufyan, leader of the Umayyads. (A minority, though, still supported Ali and his family. They became the subgroup of Muslims known as the Shia or Shiites.)

AL-ANDALUS

The rule of the Umayyad family lasted fewer than one hundred years. During the first years of the caliphate, the Umayyads were preoccupied with fighting their political and religious rivals within the Islamic Empire. But by the early 700s, they again began to send armies to spread Islam to other lands. In the west, Muslims pushed into northern Africa. There, they found converts among the local Berber tribes in Morocco. With the help of the Berbers, Arabs led by Tariq ibn Ziyad crossed the Strait of Gibraltar and seized much of what is now southern and western Spain. Once under Muslim control, this area became known as al-Andalus, which means "to become green at the end of the summer."

Despite the Umayyads' success in expanding the empire, many Muslims still held them in suspicion. The Shiites and other groups continued to question the legitimacy of their rule. The Umayyads repeatedly had to put down uprisings, which only emboldened their enemies.

In 750, one group, the Abbasids, finally succeeded in overthrowing the Umayyads in Baghdad. (The Abbasids claimed descent from Muhammad's uncle al-Abbas ibn Abd al-Muttalib.) After defeating the Umayyads' armies in several battles, the Abbasids killed the last Umayyad caliph and his family. However, one Umayyad prince, Abd al-Rahman, managed to escape. He fled to the west, eventually finding refuge in Córdoba, the capital of al-Andalus.

THE DREAM OF A GREAT CULTURAL CENTER

The Abbasids were eager to establish the legitimacy of their caliphate. As a symbolic gesture, the second Abbasid caliph, Abu Jafar al-Mansur, moved the royal court from Damascus in what is now Syria to a brand-new city called Baghdad in present-day Iraq. He wanted the shift to represent a break with the corrupt Umayyad past and a movement toward a glorious new future under the Abbasid caliphs.

Baghdad quickly grew into a beautiful and vibrant city. At its height in the ninth century, it was home to as many as one million people, an astounding population for any urban area at that time. But the Abbasids were determined to make Baghdad into something more than just a huge

The caliphs al-Mansur and al-Mamun founded the House of Wisdom in an effort to establish Baghdad as a center of culture and academics. The House of Wisdom was made up of the greatest minds in the Islamic world.

city. They wanted it to be the greatest cultural center, not just in the Islamic Empire, but in the world.

There was good reason to believe Baghdad could become the capital of world culture. Because of their conquests, Muslims had gained access to the scholarly and artistic traditions of an array of ancient civilizations. They possessed the literature and political scholarship of Persia, the medical and mathematical knowledge of India, the legal reasoning of the Romans, and the scientific and philosophical inquiries of the Greeks.

THE HOUSE OF WISDOM

Under the rule of al-Mansur, scholars began to translate Indian and Greek works. However it was his successor, Abu al-Abbas Abd Allah al-Mamun, who initiated a stunningly ambitious translation movement. He brought the greatest Islamic scholars to Baghdad to examine and translate the learning of the ancient world into Arabic. The Abbasids would commit a huge amount of money and time—about two hundred years—to this project.

As part of the translation movement, a research center called the House of Wisdom was estalished in Baghdad in 830. Under the direction of Hunayn bin Ishaq, scholars collected every manuscript they could find of each work and studied them to establish a definitive text before even beginning their translation. Many of the translators were Christians from the area of present-day Syria. They translated the Greek text into Syriac, then other translators would translate the Syriac text into Arabic.

Before the translation movement, the only book written in Arabic was the Quran. (There was, however, a tradition of oral poetry in the Arabic language.) Although Arabic had a very simple vocabulary, it proved a remarkably good language for the communication of new ideas and abstract thoughts. As a result, it became the common language among intellectuals throughout the Islamic Empire, even among non-Arabs and non-Muslims.

The translation movement preserved many works that might have otherwise been lost. For instance, the works of the Greek philosophers Plato and Aristotle had largely been forgotten by the time the project began. Only a few fragments of their works existed in all of present-day Europe.

But Muslim scholars did more than mechanically record the literature of ancient cultures for future generations. They actively evaluated these works, interpreting them to find knowledge that they could

The scholars at the House of Wisdom were tasked with identifying the definitive texts in various disciplines. They then would translate the texts into Arabic. From there, many of these academics went on to their own scholarship, often interpreted through the filter of their Muslim beliefs.

use and, even more difficult, that they could incorporate into their culture in ways that did not conflict with the Islamic worldview. For Muslim intellectuals, theologians, and philosophers, these questions prompted debates that would continue for centuries.

CÓRDOBA RIVALS BAGHDAD

During the Abbasid era, other cities in the Islamic empire became cultural centers. But perhaps Baghdad's greatest cultural rival was Córdoba, where the Umayyad prince Abd al-Rahman fled after the massacre of his family. There, Abd al-Rahman built an army. Calling himself the emir (commander) of Muslim Spain, he took control of al-Andalus.

In 756, he established an Umayyad government in the region that lasted nearly three hundred years. In 932, Abd al-Rahman III, the seventh Umayyad ruler of al-Andalus, promoted himself from emir to caliph, a direct challenge to the authority of the Abbasid rulers in Baghdad. Thereafter, the Umayyads maintained that they were the true rulers of the Islamic Empire and that its true capital was Córdoba.

For centuries, the Umayyads of Córdoba and the Abbasids of Baghdad were political rivals. Even so, scholars freely traveled between the two cities, introducing Córdoba to the books and ideas circulating in Baghdad. Al-Hakam II, also known as al-Mustansir Billah, the successor of Abd al-Rahman III, actively encouraged the importation of translations from the east. Under his reign (961–976), Córdoba emerged as a great center for learning. The city's library had more than 400,000 books, an amazingly large collection. A well-educated man himself, al-Hakam filled his court with scholars, philosophers, and artists.

Al-Hakam's patronage certainly helped make Córdoba an incubator for new ideas. But the city's long tradition of tolerance also contributed to its free-flowing intellectual atmosphere. Under the Umayyads, the people of Córdoba were subject to Islamic rule and law. But the Umayyads generally did not persecute people of other faiths. They were especially tolerant of Jews and Christians, who like Muslims worshipped a single god. Jews and Christians were subject to special taxes and had to worship in private. But otherwise, they were largely left to live as they chose, and many even embraced aspects of Islamic culture, particularly the Arabic language. These peoples were a vital part of Cordoban society, adding their own perspectives to the vibrant multilingual and multicultural mix of the city at its height.

A PERIOD OF UPHEAVAL

After al-Hakam's brief fifteen-year reign, his eleven-year-old son, Hisham II, became the new caliph in 976. However, real power over al-Andalus fell into the hands of the caliph's counselor, Abu Amir al-Mansur. Leading as a dictator, al-Mansur ordered the burning of some of the books in the Córdoba library, because he maintained that the ideas they contained were dangerous. But most of al-Mansur's energy was devoted to battling small Christian kingdoms to the north. To aid his military campaigns, al-Mansur hired Berber soldiers from North Africa. The Cordobans greatly resented the fact that these foreign troops had been unleashed throughout their lands.

When al-Mansur died in 1002, power over al-Andalus passed on to his two sons. During the second

LA MEZQUITA

In his final years, Abd al-Rahman began work on a great project to bring further and lasting glory to Córdoba. He ordered the construction of a large mosque, a Muslim house of worship. The emir's great mosque was to be a symbol of Córdoba's claim to being the new cultural center in the Islamic world.

The architecture of the Great Mosque echoed that of another structure—the mosque the Umayyad dynasty built in Damascus when it had ruled the Muslim empire. But Córdoba's mosque also incorporated local materials, including pillars salvaged from Roman ruins. By bringing together the old and new, the building celebrated both the Umayyads' distinguished past in the East and the dynasty's renewed power under Abd al-Rahman in the West.

The project of building the Great Mosque continued long after Abd al-Rahman's death. For the next two hundred years, Umayyad emirs and caliphs added onto the mosque as Córdoba expanded and its population grew. The Great Mosque, or La Mezquita (the Mosque) as it is known, became a vast structure, with horseshoe-shaped arches decorated with alternating bands of red brick and white stone and columns made of jasper, marble, granite, and onyx. La Mezquita's walls were adorned with intricate mosaics.

In 1236, a Christian army led by Ferdinand III of Castile invaded Córdoba. Seeing that the Great Mosque remained the most visible monument to Islamic rule, the Christians might have destroyed it. But instead Ferdinand entered the mosque and reconsecrated it as a Christian church. In the sixteenth century, the mosque was converted into a cathedral. Today, it remains a destination for thousands of tourists interested in Spain's Muslim past.

son's reign, the Andalusians had enough. They rebelled in 1009, and the heirs to the Umayyad dynasty were restored to the caliphate. But it was too late to return to the old order. The Umayyads gradually lost their hold on the region. The caliphate officially came to an end in 1031, as al-Andalus disintegrated into a collection of some sixty city-states, called *taifas*. The rulers of these small kingdoms fought one another constantly, all jockeying for more power.

One such king, Mutamid of Seville, asked for military aid from the Almoravids, leaders of an Islamic religious movement. These conservative Muslim Berbers were building an empire in north Africa, with its capital in Marrakesh. Once in

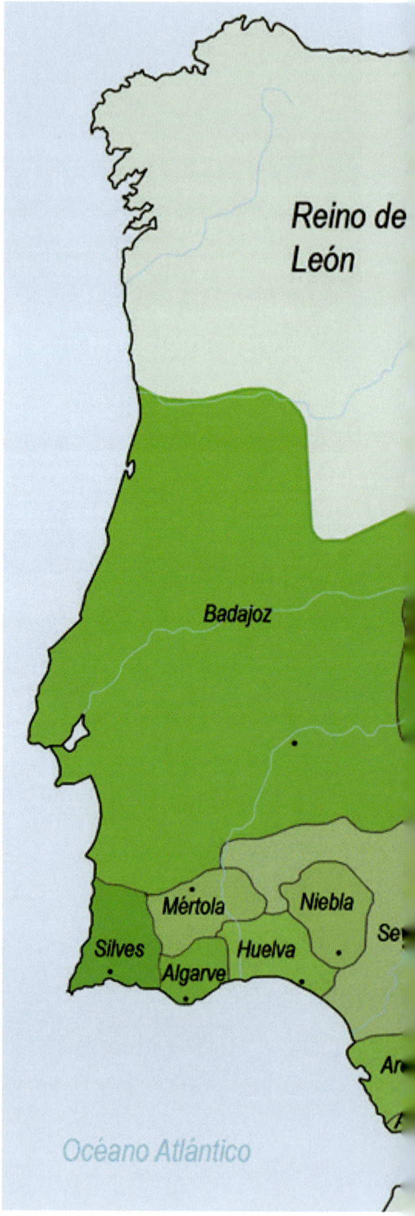

Nearly one century before Averroes's birth, al-Andalus experienced major upheaval. After the collapse of the Umayyad caliphate of Córdoba in 1031, al-Andalus was divided into dozens of *taifas*, or city-states.

al-Andalus, they seized the region and incorporated it into their empire. The Almoravids ruled al-Andalus until 1146, when it was taken over by the Almohads, an even more extreme fundamentalist Muslim sect of Berber invaders.

It was into this world that Averroes was born in 1126. Politically and culturally, al-Andalus was experiencing upheaval. The tolerant society centered in Córdoba under the Umayyad caliphate was becoming a distant memory, as the Almoravids imposed a much more restrictive and conservative view of Islam on the Andalusians. But even in this relatively repressive environment, Averroes would grow up around scholars, philosophers, theologians, jurists, and scientists—all searching for means of understanding the universe and the place of humans within it. From their works and teachings, Averroes would build an intellectual foundation on which he could construct his own philosophy.

CHAPTER TWO

THE EDUCATION OF AVERROES

Although Averroes made many important contributions that still resonate today, there is much we do not know about him. Al-Marrakushi and Ibn Abi Usaybi penned biographies of Averroes in the thirteenth century that provide a few clues about his personality. For instance, his biographers suggest that he was fiercely loyal to his tight circle of friends. As one biographer explained, Averroes took criticism of his own work in stride, but when a poet wrote a satire about one of his companions, Averroes became so angry he struck the poet. Averroes was also said to be a perfectionist. One story told of how Averroes, as an older man, destroyed some love poems he had composed in his youth, not because they were embarrassing, but because they were badly written. Averroes's biographers also portrayed him as an incredibly diligent scholar. One biographer noted that Averroes worked every night of his life, reading and writing, except for the day he got married and the day his father died.

The mosque Imam Malik, Ville Nouvelle, in Fes, Morocco, is named for Malik ibn Anas al-Asbahi, one of the most respected scholars of Muslim law. Averroes's grandfather had studied Maliki law, and Averroes, in turn, studied his grandfather's work.

A DISTINGUISHED LINEAGE

None of Averroes's biographers, however, wrote about his earliest years. His family background, though, gives a sense of how he was raised and how he was educated. Averroes was born into one of the most important and influential families in al-Andalus. His father was a religious judge, or *qadi*. His grandfather was even more distinguished. He was the qadi and *iman* (a religious leader) of the Great Mosque of Córdoba, one of the city's most beautiful houses of worship. Given his lineage, Averroes was certainly schooled in Islamic law so he would be qualified to follow in their footsteps.

Undoubtedly, Averroes's education included studying his grandfather's work. He was a follower of the Maliki, a school of Islamic law that originated in Medina in the eighth century. Its founder, Malik ibn Anas al-Asbahi (about 713–795), wrote *Al-Muwatta* (The Straight Path), the earliest surviving book of Muslim laws. Averroes is said to have known Al-Muwatta by heart.

Averroes's grandfather took a relatively open-minded approach to the study of law. Some in the Maliki school did not think that humans should use reason to study the principles of law in the Quran. Averroes's grandfather, however, disagreed. As quoted in Roger Arnaldez's *Averroes: A Rationalist in Islam* (2000), Averroes's grandfather once wrote, "God is known only through speculation regarding the signs of proof that He has made available in order that He might be known and that they might be used as proof. But only he who has reason capable of speculating and proving is able to speculate and carry out the proof."

Claudius Galenus, better known as Galen, was an ancient Greek physician and philosopher. Galen's revolutionary medical research influenced generations of scientists, including Averroes.

Averroes benefitted from the scholarship of earlier Islamic academics, including the philosopher al-Kindi.

MEDICAL STUDIES

Averroes also was a student of medicine. One of his teachers was Abu Jafar ibn Harun al-Tarjali, a learned physician who was the personal doctor of an Almohad caliph. A contemporary of al-Tarjali glowingly described his talents as a physician and a scholar, according to Arnaldez's *Averroes*: "[al-Tarjali] was among the most important inhabitants of Seville, an accomplished philosopher, established in this field, passionate about the works of Aristotle and other early philosophers, excellent and distinguished in the art of medicine, experienced in its foundations and applications, a good practitioner in the treatment of the ill, praiseworthy in the application of his methods."

During his early medical studies, Averroes was certainly exposed to the work of the Greek physician Galen (about 129–199). Living in the second century, Galen was the most important medical writer in the ancient world. He wrote numerous treatises on anatomy, pharmacology, and diagnosis, as well as a work of philosophy, *On Medical Experience*.

Averroes was also interested in mathematics and science as a young man. He was particularly drawn to astronomy and probably was engaged in some scientific research in this area. Averroes once expressed regret that he did not have enough time to make a study of the movement of heavenly bodies. As he explained, according to Arnaldez in *Averroes*, "In my youth I was hoping that it would be possible to bring this research to fruition; but at the advanced age where I presently am, I have lost hope."

ISLAMIC INTERPRETATION OF GREEK PHILOSOPHY

Growing up in the intellectually rich atmosphere of Córdoba, Averroes was undoubtedly educated in past and contemporary schools of Islamic philosophy, although none of his biographers list his philosophy teachers by name. Philosophy—the study of the nature of reality and principles underlying thinking and being—originated in ancient Greece in the sixth century BCE. Long before Averroes's birth, many of the

CLASSICAL PHILOSOPHY

Philosophy in the Western world has been shaped in large part by three ancient Greeks—Socrates, Plato, and Aristotle.

Socrates (469–399 BCE) was a great teacher. In Athens, he taught his students by asking them questions, then asking more pointed questions based on the implications of their answers. This teaching method is now known as the Socratic Method. Angering both religious and political leaders, Socrates was convicted of corrupting Athens' youth. He willingly accepted his sentence of death by drinking poison.

Socrates left behind no writings. His student Plato (about 427–347 BCE) is responsible for recording what is known of his philosophy. Plato wrote and taught at the Academy, which he founded near Athens in 386. His writings were in the form of dialogues and covered a wide range of subjects, from law to mathematics. He argued that there were Ideas, or Forms, that had an independent reality and never changed. His most famous book is The Republic, which discusses the qualities of a just state.

Plato's most famous student was Aristotle (384-322 BCE). Son of the physician to the Macedonian king, Aristotle became the tutor of Alexander the Great. In 335 BCE, Aristotle established a school, the Athenian Lyceum, which became one of the leading centers of learning in the ancient world. His philosophy concentrated on the systematic use of logic to discern unchanging principles that form the basis of all knowledge. Like Socrates, Aristotle faced criminal charges for teaching philosophy. He was forced to flee Athens to the city of Chalcis a year before his death.

most important works of Greek philosophy had been translated into Arabic in Baghdad, and these translated works had been imported to Córdoba. Also at Averroes's disposal were the writings of early Islamic philosophers, which contained their thoughts on the works of the ancient Greeks, particularly Plato and Aristotle.

The first Islamic scholar to embrace Greek philosophy was Yaqub ibn Ishaq al-Sabah al-Kindi (about 805–870). Producing more than 300 books, al-Kindi wrote on a wide range of subjects, including mathematics, logic, psychology, and astrology. But his most memorable work concentrated on the value of studying Plato and Aristotle. Among his books was *The Quantity of the Books of Aristotle* and *What is Required for the Acquisition of Philosophy*.

At the time, Islamic traditionalists were suspicious of Greek philosophy. They maintained that, as the work of pagans and foreigners, it provided nothing useful to the devout Muslim. Al-Kindi argued that the true seeker of truth had the duty to use whatever tools were available, "even if it were to come from distant races and nations different from us." Furthermore, al-Kindi claimed that Greek philosophy was not in conflict with the Islamic faith. On the contrary, he wrote that the tools of rational thought offered by the Greeks could

Al-Farabi was a philosopher, scientist, mathematician, and scholar of music theory. His influence on Averroes was as a philosopher. Al-Farabi's rationalist views relied on reason and intellect over the senses. Many saw this as contrary to Muslim beliefs.

actually be used to confirm the articles of faith revealed by the Quran.

ISLAMIC NEOPLATONISM

The development of Islamic philosophy was also shaped by Abu Nasr al-Farabi. Al-Farabi was the founder of Islamic Neoplatonism. Neoplatonism was a branch of philosophy that originated in Alexandria, an Egyptian city founded by Alexander the Great in 330 and captured by Arabs in 641. Neoplatonism was first developed by Plotinus, a Greek-Egyptian philosopher who, during the third century CE, attempted to reconcile Greek philosophy with Eastern religious traditions.

The name Neoplatonism refers to Plato. But Plotinus's school of thought also drew from other Greek writers, including Aristotle and Pythagoras. It embraced elements of Judaism and Christianity as well. Neoplatonists believed that all existence came from a single source, the One, with which individual souls could mystically be united.

For al-Farabi, the ultimate goal of humanity was to achieve happiness. He felt that happiness was not achievable in isolation, but possible only within the realm of human society. He envisioned the "virtuous city" as the ideal state in which humans could find

Avicenna made remarkable contributions to philosophy and medicine. Avicenna's influence was far-reaching, and his work most definitely would have influenced Averroes.

happiness. Because of these theories, al-Farabi is now considered the first political philosopher of the Islamic world.

Before Averroes, the most important of the Islamic philosophers was Ibn Sina, better known by his Latin name Avicenna. Born in Persia, Avicenna was considered a genius both in medicine and in philosophy. In his multivolume *Canon of Medicine*, he collected the medical knowledge of the Greeks, Arabs, and Romans, producing a text that would be consulted by physicians for centuries. As a philosopher, Avicenna was influenced by Neoplatonism, though his work concentrated on Aristotle. Like al-Farabi, Avicenna advanced an emanationist theory about the creation of the world, in which God was the starting point for a series of causes and effects that make up the structure of reality. Although in some respects his philosophy resembled al-Farabi's, Avicenna was a far more fluid writer, and his work reached a much larger readership.

Also central to Averroes's philosophical education was Ibn Bajjah, who was also known as Avempace. Avempace was the first major Islamic writer in al-Andalus to delve into philosophy. He wrote paraphrases of Aristotle and interpretations of al-Farabi's work, for whom he had great respect. Avempace paid a price for his intellectual adventures. Islamic traditionalists who opposed his writings had him imprisoned for heresy, or holding a belief contrary to accepted religious doctrine. He was freed only after Averroes's grandfather intervened.

AL-GHAZALI

For many centuries, Islamic scholars had questioned whether philosophy could be reconciled with Muslim belief. But one of the most significant and sophisticated examinations of the matter was written a few decades before Averroes's birth by Abu Hamid al-Ghazali (about 1058–1111). A Persian, al-Ghazali was a learned theologian fully versed in the beliefs of the Neoplatonists, which he summarized in his book *Intentions of the Philosophers.* His command of the subject made his ultimate attack on the Neoplatonism, which was popularized by al-Farabi and Avicenna, all the more devastating.

In *Incoherence of the Philosophers* (*Tuhafut al-Falasifa*), al-Ghazali conceded that some aspects of Greek-Arab philosophy were useful paths to knowledge. He singled out logic and mathematics, since he did not see them in conflict with religious truth. But al-Ghazali condemned metaphysics—the branch of philosophy that deals with the nature of reality—as wholly incompatible with Islam. He argued that the Quran presents an all-powerful God, without whom man is nothing. Al-Ghazali condemned the Neoplatonists for challenging the transcendence of God by subjecting him to categories of human thought.

Al-Ghazali's book was a landmark in Islamic thought. In large part because of *Incoherence of the Philosophers*, the study of Greek philosophy fell out of favor in the western portions of the Islamic Empire. Almost certainly, Averroes read it as part of his early education.

IBN TUFAYL

Of Averroes's contemporaries, the philosopher who had the most influence on Averroes was Abu Bakr ibn Tufayl. Ibn Tufayl helped revive Neoplatonism in Muslim Spain through his book *Risalat Hayy ibn Yaqzan (Living Son of the Awake)*, a philosophical novel. It told the story of a man trapped alone on a desert island. Through observation and thought, Ibn Tufayl's character was able to discover truths about God and the world.

However, to Ibn Tufayl, philosophical contemplation ultimately fell short. He believed a soul could not be united with the One without a mystical emptying out of the self. This idea showed Ibn Tufayl's sympathy for the Islamic religious movement known as Sufism.

As an adult, Averroes was friendly with Ibn Tufayl, although he had little affinity for the mystical aspects of his philosophy. Ibn Tufayl's great influence over Averroes's life did not come from his work, but from his connections. It was Ibn Tufayl who introduced Averroes to his patron, the caliph Abu Yaqub Yusuf, thus setting in motion Averroes's brilliant career in philosophy.

CHAPTER THREE

PHILOSOPHY AND ISLAM

As a patron, Abu Yaqub Yusuf made sure Averroes was well taken care of. The caliph appointed the scholar to a series of extremely prestigious posts. First, he made Averroes a qadi, or judge, in the Andalusian city of Seville. A few years later, Yusuf afforded his philosopher an even greater honor, naming him the grand qadi, or chief judge, of his beloved Córdoba. This appointment no doubt had special meaning for Averroes, since his esteemed grandfather had once held the position. In 1182, Yusuf paid further tribute to Averroes by making him his personal physician, a position previously held by Averroes's friend and mentor Ibn Tufayl.

These years were busy for Averroes, as he often traveled between Marrakesh, Córdoba, and Seville in order to fulfill his official duties as a judge and physician. But, despite his active public life, he was also engulfed in the private world of scholarship. In 1169,

Averroes began his great commentaries on Aristotle. This work was a massive endeavor, but he continued to write on a wide variety of other topics. Some of his most important works at this time were his books about theology, in which he made a passionate, rational argument for the essential compatibility of Aristotelian philosophy and Muslim thought.

THE ENDURING PHILOSOPHY OF ARISTOTLE

Born in 384 BCE, Aristotle was an influential thinker even in his day. For twenty years, he studied with Plato, the greatest Greek philosopher before him. Plato taught that true knowledge, an understanding of the essence of things, could only come to the contemplative soul who turns away from the world. Driven by an overriding interest in understanding the material world around him, Aristotle in contrast valued the knowledge humans could obtain by using their senses.

Aristotle proposed an ordered, systematic study of the world, creating categories of study, such as biology and physics, that continue to be used by scholars today. His own writings about the natural world included *Physics*, *Meteorology*, and *History of Animals*. In general, Aristotle had an enormous impact on all sciences by encouraging the idea of expanding scientific knowledge through direct observation. Aristotle also wrote about the art of public speaking in *Rhetoric* and analyzed literature in *Poetics*. In the field of philosophy, one of Aristotle's greatest contributions was a system of reasoning called logic. In fact, in the Islamic world, Aristotle was often called Sahib al-Mantiq, Arabic for "Master of Logic." Central to Aristotle's system of logical reasoning was the syllogism. In a syllogism, two statements, called premises, logically lead to a third, known as a conclusion. For instance, Aristotle himself provided this example: If all humans are mortal and all Greeks are humans, then all Greeks are mortal.

In his *Metaphysics*, Aristotle presented his theory of the nature of reality. In a departure from Plato, Aristotle insisted that the study of metaphysics must begin in an investigation of what humans could learn from their senses, then move from that point to abstract thought. In this work, Aristotle also presented God as the highest form of being, pure intelligence without material form. Aristotle thought the world had always existed, just as God had always existed. The world was neither created nor consciously controlled by God, who did not affect day-to-day events. Aristotle also held that humans were the only creatures with an intelligence resembling that of God's. It was therefore man's highest calling to devote himself to reasoned thought.

AVERROES'S COMMENTARIES ON ARISTOTLE

Averroes approached Aristotle's work by writing commentaries in three different lengths—short, medium, and long. The short commentaries were little more than paraphrases of the originals. The long commentaries were lengthy scholarly discourses, often devoting pages to explain a short passage. Some later writers dismissed Averroes's work as just slavish rewordings of Aristotle's writings. But Averroes's most sophisticated commentaries were

Among his other areas of focus, Averroes studied Artistotle extensively. He wrote commentaries of varying depth about the ancient Greek philosopher's writings. Despite many challenges in reading and interpreting Aristotle's works, Averroes used them to define his own original theories.

PLATO'S *REPUBLIC*

Aristotle wrote a treatise titled *Politics*, which is now one of his most widely read works. Averroes, however, never wrote a commentary on this book, because, in his words, it "has not fallen into our hands." It was the only major work of Aristotle's that was not translated into Arabic in Averroes's lifetime. Averroes, though, was able to paraphrase another great discussion of politics from the ancient world—*The Republic* by Plato.

Plato's *Republic* dealt with the question of what justice is and how people should be governed. In it, Plato explained his notion of the ideal government, which would be ruled by a philosopher-king. *The Republic* also presented the theory that human society could change and even be perfected.

In Averroes's world, many of the ideas in *The Republic* were considered controversial, if not dangerous. The rulers of al-Andalus did not want average people to wonder if their government could be improved. And they certainly did not want people to ponder whether the social order that placed the rulers at the top was something that could be changed.

truly original works. While illuminating Aristotle's thinking, they also provided unique interpretations that give us a view into Averroes's own personal philosophical beliefs.

Interpreting Aristotle's teachings was certainly a formidable task. As Averroes's patron Abu Yaqub Yusuf had discovered, Aristotle was a complex thinker whose meaning was often hard to discern. About thirty works of Aristotle survive, which amount to less than a quarter of the writings he produced. Many of the extant writings are not polished works meant for publication. They were probably lecture notes. Not surprisingly, some passages in these works are highly repetitive, while the language in others is confoundingly terse or obscure. The material was probably put in sequence by ancient editors rather than by Aristotle himself, making them all the more confusing.

In interpreting Aristotle, Averroes faced an additional obstacle—the translations he had to work with. Averroes did not study Aristotle's original Greek texts, but instead he worked from Arabic versions. Their translators had an imperfect knowledge of the ancient Greek language. As a result, the Arabic translations were often at best muddled and at worst outright inaccurate. In making his commentaries, Averroes had to constantly compare the various translations he had access to. For many passages, he had to decide which translation seemed the most reliable. His writings often alluded to choices he had had to make and offered justifications for them.

Averroes faced still another challenge in his commentaries. A number of Arabic translations wrongly attributed to Aristotle works that were in fact written by two later Greek philosophers, Plotinus and Proclus, both proponents of Neoplatonism. One of Averroes's goals was in essence to purify the Islamic texts of Aristotelian philosophy by sorting out those ideas that were genuinely Aristotle's from those inserted into his work by later thinkers. By repeatedly pointing out passages that he believed were inconsistent with Aristotle's core beliefs, Averroes hoped to present a truer version of Aristotle's philosophy than had previously been available in the Islamic world.

ARISTOTLE'S INFLUENCE ON AVERROES'S OWN WRITINGS

The influence of Aristotle is evident in much of Averroes's other writings, including his works about Islamic theology. These included *Decisive Treatise on the Relation of Philosophy* and *Religion and Exposition*

Ancient Greek philosopher Plotinus was a Neoplatonist. Some of the texts Averroes studied were not in fact written by Aristotle but instead by Plotinus. Thus, Averroes set out to correct the Islamic versions of the ancient Greek texts.

of the Methods of Proof. His best known religious work, however, was *Incoherence of the Incoherence.*

The title was a clever play on *Incoherence of the Philosophers*, written by the famous Islamic theologian Abu Hamid al-Ghazali. In the late eleventh century, al-Ghazali was instrumental in the spread of Sufism. Followers of this Islamic religious movement sought union with God through prayer.

Al-Ghazali's *Incoherence of the Philosophers* had a deep influence on Islamic thought with its devastating critique of Greek philosophy. He argued that philosophy presented theories that were fundamentally at odds with Islamic principles by meticulously examining twenty questions discussed by the philosophers. Al-Ghazali then concluded that, for a devout Muslim, the philosophers' answers to these questions amounted to heresy.

A large element of al-Ghazali's attack was his insistence that, even if philosophy did not contradict Islam, as a system of thought it was so incoherent that it was utterly useless as a tool for studying the world. While making this argument, al-Ghazali hoped to destroy the influence of Avicenna. At the time the book was written, Avicenna was the leading Islamic proponent of the philosophy of the ancient Greeks.

The Muslim theologian Abu Hamid al-Ghazali offered an important critique of ancient Greek philosophy. Al-Ghazali's belief was that Greek philosophy was inherently at odds with Islam.

This page is from a twelfth-century edition of the Quran. Averroes disagreed with al-Ghazali that the philosophies developed by the ancient Greeks could not be reconciled with the holy text of Muslim theology.

Just as al-Ghazali's *Incoherence of the Philosophers* was a direct attack on Avicenna, Averroes's *Incoherence* was meant to be a direct attack on al-Ghazali. Averroes took on al-Ghazali point by point, offering a thorough defense of Aristotle. Averroes condemned al-Ghazali for denouncing philosophy, which he celebrated as a valid and valuable means for examining God and the world.

In writing *Incoherence*, Averroes had another goal as well. He wanted his readership to reexamine the work of Avicenna and other earlier Islamic philosophers, who he believed had misunderstood Aristotle. This was in part because they blindly followed the flawed Arabic translations containing elements of Neoplatonist beliefs. But Averroes was also very critical of many of Avicenna's interpretations. Just as in his commentaries Averroes wanted to purify Aristotle from outside influences, in *Incoherence* he wanted to purify Islamic philosophy from ideas that misrepresented Aristotle's work.

DIVERGING FROM ARISTOTLE

One of Averroes's central arguments with al-Ghazali dealt with the origin of the world. According to al-Ghazali,

Aristotle maintained that the world was eternal. For Aristotle, there could not have been a time when God existed but the world did not, since time is a measure of changing events, and there could be no changing events without the world.

Al-Ghazali devoted much of his book to the question of the world's origin. He claimed that the philosopher's view contradicted Islam, because several passages of the Quran suggest that God created the world. In the traditional Islamic view, the world was created *ex nihilo* (that is, out of nothing) and was kept in existence only through God's will and power.

Averroes felt that al-Ghazali misrepresented Aristotle, whose beliefs, in his eyes, were actually entirely reconcilable with the Quran. According to Averroes's interpretation, the philosopher believed the world was neither eternal nor created in time, but that it was created from eternity. He attacked al-Ghazali's contention that creation could have occurred in time because it brought into question God's omnipotence. If God were all powerful, how could there have been a time before which he could not create the world? And if he could create it at any time, why would he have chosen the time he did?

DIVINE KNOWLEDGE

Aristotle argued that God can only think "of what is most divine and precious." He maintained it was unworthy of God to know of mundane matters, asking, "Are there not some things about which it is incredible that it [God] should think?" To al-Ghazali, this belief meant that God's knowledge and power was limited. Since the God of the Quran had unlimited power, he believed that all philosophers should be branded as infidels.

Similarly, al-Ghazali spoke out against Aristotle's contention that God did not play a role in day-to-day affairs of the world. He explained that to human beings there may seem to be a consistent and unalterable pattern of causes that create certain effects, but God, being all-powerful, could change that at any time. Al-Ghazali argued that, in fact, the miracles descripbed in the Quran are this kind of intervention. For instance, people expect an object that comes into contact with fire to burn. But the Quran recounts that when Abraham's enemies tried to kill him by setting him aflame, the fire did not burn him. In this case, God intervened in the world in a way that altered the expected pattern of cause and effect.

For Averroes, al-Ghazali's criticism boiled the argument down to whether God knows only universal truths or knows all particulars of life on earth. Averroes argued that this discussion was fundamentally flawed because it made the mistake of comparing God's knowledge to human knowledge. He said that divine knowledge and human knowledge have to be radically different. Human knowledge, after all, comes from examining the effect of a thing known. Divine knowledge, on the other hand, is the cause of the thing known. To Averroes, it is part of God's mystery that human beings cannot understand divine knowledge.

PHILOSOPHY AND THE QURAN

In al-Ghazali's opinion, the nature of the afterlife was another area in which philosophy was in conflict with Islam. The Greek philosophers accepted the existence of the soul after the death of the body, though they generally rejected the idea that this soul has a physical presence. As al-Ghazali pointed out at length, this idea seemed in direct contrast to the Quran, which presented graphic accounts of the life both good and bad Muslims could expect after death. Since the afterlife included bodily sensations, al-Ghazali maintained that scripture made it clear that the soul was reunited with a body after death. He asked, "What is the objection to admitting the conjunction of both spiritual and bodily pleasures as well as corresponding miseries?"

Averroes was not troubled by this apparent contradiction. He suggested that the afterlife depicted in the Quran was intended to impress upon common people the necessity of living good lives. Averroes believed that only a small number of people were capable of choosing to live correctly merely because it was the right thing to do. Everyone else required the lure of eternal rewards or the threat of eternal punishment.

Averroes pointed out that the Quran itself acknowledges that it should be read on different levels. In several passages, the Quran notes that most of its verses are easily understood. These constitute the core of the scriptures that every Muslim can comprehend. But the Quran itself also declares that some of its verses are ambiguous, thus open to interpretation. According to Averroes, only those "well-grounded in knowledge" could truly understand these difficult verses. And for Averroes, no one could be well-grounded in knowledge without an understanding of philosophy. In his view, not only was the study of philosophy compatible with Islam, but the Quran actually encouraged its use.

CHAPTER FOUR

LAW AND MEDICINE

It is easy to forget that while Averroes was writing his philosophical works, he also had two professional jobs in the legal and medical fields.

Averroes held the post of qadi, or judge, for nearly twenty-five years. Although ultimate legal authority rested with the caliph, a qadi still had a substantial amount of power. Since there was no jury system in al-Andalus, the qadi was solely responsible for rendering verdicts and determining punishments, though on difficult cases he might consult a council of judicial experts. After Averroes was promoted to grand qadi of Córdoba, he was also charged with appointing the qadis for outlying areas.

DIVINE LAW

Despite their considerable authority, the qadis had restrictions on their legal decisions. They had to apply the Sharia, or religious law. The Sharia was composed of laws said to be imparted to Muslims through divine revelation. These include about 350 verses scattered throughout the Quran that deal with legal issues. Divine law was also found in the Sunna. This was a body of teachings, recorded by Muhammad's early followers, based on things the Prophet said and did. For a qadi, the rules set out in the Quran and Sunna could not be questioned, since they were considered the word of God.

The Sharia, however, did not deal with every possible legal problem that could arise. For issues it did not address directly, the qadi turned to *fiqh*. Fiqh consisted of rules for appropriate human conduct that had been compiled by men using their reasoning. Fiqh did not have same authority as the Sharia because it was the work of humans, not God.

The proper application of Islamic law was long the subject of debate among scholars. By the time Averroes became a qadi, several different schools of law had emerged. The most liberal was the Hanafi, which allowed judges some room to interpret law based on the use of specific intellectual tools. For instance, if the Sharia did not apply directly to a specific case, a Hanafi qadi could make a ruling based on custom or even on his own judicial preference.

Averroes was trained in the Maliki school, which was more conservative. But it still allowed qadis some flexibility. A Maliki qadi was permitted, for example, to consider the public interest in deciding a case. He could also make a ruling in order to "block the means." This meant a qadi could prevent someone brought before the court from performing a lawful act if the qadi believed it would ultimately lead to illegal behavior.

AVERROES'S *PRIMER*

Averroes wrote several treatises about Islamic law. The most extensive was *Primer of the Discretionary Scholar (Bidayat al-Mujtahid)*. The *Primer* summarized the history of the different schools of Islamic law and discussed why they each came to the conclusions they did. Unlike his writings in philosophy and theology, this work represented fairly traditional ideas. (Some scholars have even suggested that it is so conventional it could

This twelfth-century illustration of a man pleading before a *qadi* suggests what Averroes's working life entailed. In addition to his academic work, Averroes served as a *qadi*, or judge, for a quarter of a century.

Sharia law is a set of legal rules imparted to Muslims through divine revelation. In his work as a qadi, Averroes was bound to rule by Sharia law. Averroes's writings tell us that his views on the subject were uncharacteristically. traditional.

not actually have been written by Averroes.)

In the *Primer*, Averroes acknowledged the complete authority of the Sharia. He also generally supported the Maliki point of view, although he occasionally expressed opinions at variance with it. For instance, Averroes's writing strongly stressed the need for legal interpretation through reasoning. He was especially an advocate for the use of analogy, a reasoning tool first promoted by the Hanafi school. Averroes held that when there was no law from the Sharia that addressed a specific case, a qadi could rule based on a law that dealt with a matter that was similar, or analogous, to the case at hand.

One biographer of Averroes described a case he ruled on by using analogous reasoning. The students of a male professor began gossiping that their teacher was

Averroes summarized and built on Galen's work, producing twenty medical texts of his own. But, as far as historians know, he did not have practical experience as a physician until he was appointed court physician in Marrakesh.

having a romantic relationship with a handsome young man. One student even wrote a poem about the affair. As it turned out, the gossip was untrue, and the professor approached Averroes, asking him to punish the students who had spread the story. Since homosexual acts were against Muslim law, the professor claimed they had falsely accused him of a crime.

To make his judgment, Averroes referred to a story in the Quran. It told of a chaste woman who was falsely accused of a shameful act. Her accusers were punished by eighty blows from a whip. Although this case involved a wrongly accused woman instead of a wrongly accused man, Averroes found they were similar enough to justify ruling against the professor's accusers. The biographer did not record the exact punishment he ordered.

For readers of his philosophical works, Averroes's defense for using analogy in legal proceedings was familiar. In some instances, Averroes felt judges could use reasoning to settle legal disputes just as he believed that seekers of truth could use reasoning to solve theological or philosophical questions.

MEDICAL WORK

In 1182 Averroes began a third career, with his appointment as the physician to the royal court in Marrakesh. The appointment was undoubtedly a great honor. But it is not clear how much hands-on work was involved. There is no record of Averroes having been a practicing physician before his appointment. However, it is still obvious from his writings that he had an extensive background in medicine—knowledge that probably was sufficient to provide medical treatment to the caliph and his court.

In Averroes's day, there was an extensive body of medical works available in al-Andalus. Much of the information was handed down from the ancient Greeks, particularly the philosopher and physician Galen. Averroes himself produced about twenty books about medicine, most written before he became court physician. The majority were summaries and paraphrases of Galen dealing with a wide variety of topics, from fevers to medications to hygiene. Averroes also wrote a commentary on *al-Urjuzah*, a medical poem written by the Islamic philosopher Avicenna.

However, Averroes's best known medical work was *Generalities in Medicine* (*Al-Kulliyyat*, written between 1153 and 1169). In the twelfth century, it was translated into Latin and given the title *Colliget*. In this form, Averroes's work was used as a medical textbook in Europe for centuries.

GENERALITIES AND PARTICULARITIES

As the title suggests, *Generalities* was intended to provide physicians with general principles that governed the body in illness and in health. One of Averroes's biographers, Ibn Abi Usaybi (also spelled as Usaybiah), noted that the book was conceived as one part of a two-volume set. According to Arnaldez's *Averroes*, Ibn Abi Usaybi wrote, "Averroes composed his book on generalities and asked Avenzoar, to write his on particularities, so that, together, their two books would form a perfect work on the art of medicine." A friend of Averroes, Avenzoar (also known as Ibn Zuhr) had conducted medical experiments and probably had more experience dealing directly with patients. Averroes perhaps thought Avenzoar was a better choice than himself to tackle the "particularities" of medicine, that is, the day-to-day care of the human body.

Arnaldez quotes the end of *Generalities*, where Averroes wrote that "he who has mastered the generalities that we have written will be able to understand what is correct and what is erroneous in the therapeutic practice of the authors of *kunnash* [works of therapy]." But his book provided more than just guidelines for judging specific medicinal treatments. It also gave readers plenty of practical advice. It systematically discussed the body, recounting the proper workings of its various parts, how they could be affected by illness, and how these illnesses could be treated.

In keeping with the Islamic medical beliefs of his day, Averroes placed a great emphasis on keeping the body well. In fact, he defined medicine as "an effective art, based on true principles and concerned with preserving man's health and abating disease, as far as possible." Accordingly, his books often gave detailed advice about everyday matters such as nutrition and physical activity. In one work, he counseled readers to eat a balanced diet of bread, poultry, fish, and mutton, though he cautioned against eating any fruits but figs and grapes. He advised that regular exercise should take place after a meal and be followed by bathing. Averroes also maintained that in restoring health, natural methods, such as changes in diet, were generally more effective than artificial means, such as medicine and surgery. Averroes wrote, "When the physician

Avenzoar, whose real name was Ibn Zuhr, was a practicing physician and surgeon in al-Andalus. Even though he was a contemporary of Averroes, Avenzoar was a great influence on the court physician, having extensive practical experience in medicine.

treats a patient in any way at all, he is really assisting nature according to a determinate course of action and towards a determinate goal…If the physician is ignorant of that course or that goal…and treats the patient in a haphazard way, he will be essentially at fault and is right only by accident."

In general, Averroes's writings on medicine and health were the least original of his works. He drew heavily on existing medical texts, including Avicenna's famous *Canon of Medicine*, which covered a much wider breadth of knowledge than Averroes's *Generalities*. Averroes, though, did contribute to medical science by his insistence that a physician had to use reason to diagnosis illness and determine a course of treatment. Like Galen, Averroes held that one could not be a good physician without also being a good philosopher.

ADVICE FROM THE MEDICAL EXPERT

Throughout *Generalities in Medicine*, Averroes offers practical advice about how to maintain one's health. He is especially generous with dietary advice, some of which sounds as though it could have been written by a nutritionist today. In this excerpt from Caroline Stone's 2003 article entitled "Doctor, Philosopher, Renaissance Man," Averroes extols the healthful benefits of cooking with olive oil:

> When [oil] comes from ripe, healthy olives and its properties have not been tempered with artificially, it can be assimilated perfectly by the human body. Food seasoned with olive oil is nutritious, provided the oil is fresh and not rancid. Generally speaking, all olive oil is excellent for people and for that reason in [al-Andalus] it is the only medium needed for cooking meat, given that the best way of preparing it is what we call braising. This is how it is done: Take oil and pour it in a cooking pot. Place the meat in it and then add hot water, a little at a time, simmering it without letting it boil.

CHAPTER FIVE

REMEMBERING AVERROES

Abu Yaqub Yusuf's patronage of Averroes finally came to an end in 1184 at his death. The caliph had supported Averroes's scholarship and professional career for fifteen years. Yusuf was succeeded by his son, Abu Yusaf Yaqub al-Mansur, who continued to be Averroes's patron for the next decade.

PUNISHMENT

Eleven years into his reign, al-Mansur suddenly turned on Averroes, who was now almost seventy years old. The caliph banished both the philosopher and his followers from the court. Furthermore, Averroes was forbidden to write about philosophy, politics, and religions, and many of his books were burned. It is not certain exactly what happened between Averroes and al-Mansur. Biographer Ibn Abi Usaybi speculated that Averroes had offended al-Mansur by referring to him in print as the king of the Berbers, since Berbers in Arabic could be used to mean "barbarians."

More likely, though, politics played the biggest role in the caliph's attack on Averroes. At the time, al-Mansur was battling Christians in present-day Spain and was desperate for the support of Maliki judges, who still held great sway among the people. Even though Averroes himself was a Maliki qadi, more conservative judges held him in suspicion because of his embrace of philosophy and philosophers. In fact, records suggest that some enemies of philosophy were calling for Averroes to be put to death.

In the end, Averroes's punishment was far less severe. After his banishment, he was probably confined to a home in al-Isalah (now Lucena) near Córdoba in a fairly comfortable version of house arrest. Nevertheless, Averroes's banishment must have been a painful experience. His personal reputation was sullied, and he was publicly branded as a bad Muslim. At least once during his exile, he was chased away from a Córdoba mosque by a furious mob.

After two years, the caliph recalled Averroes to Marrakesh. The ban on Averroes's writings was also lifted, although it appears that the elderly philosopher wrote nothing after returning to the Almohad capital. Averroes remained in the caliph's good graces until his death on December 11, 1198. Three months later, in accordance with his wishes, his body was laid to rest in Córdoba. According to Stone's article, "Doctor, Philosopher, Renaissance Man," an eyewitness wrote about Averroes's funeral: "When the coffin with his body was laid upon the bier [coffin stand], they put his works on the opposite side to serve as a counterweight. I was standing there…and I said to myself, 'On one side the master and on the other his works.'"

Historians are not exactly certain of the reason, but after a long relationship, al-Mamun banished Averroes. In addition, Averroes's writings were banned and his books destroyed. Averroes's banishment, which lasted two years, is depicted in this illustration.

AL-ANDALUS FADES FROM GREATNESS

Averroes's many friends and associates mourned his passing. But in the years following his death, his reputation suffered in the Islamic world. Some scholars denigrated his work, perhaps none as pointedly as the philosopher Ibn Sabin. Dismissing Averroes as "merely an imitator of Aristotle," Ibn Sabin wrote that "he was a man of limited scope, faint understanding, foolish conceptions and lacking in intuition."

More commonly, though, Averroes's writings were merely ignored by Islamic scholars. After Averroes's death, philosophy in general fell into disrepute among Muslims. Averroes may have laid a foundation for Islamic philosophy in al-Andalus, but in subsequent years, no one bothered to build upon it. Interest in theology, however, continued to grow. While Averroes's work was largely dismissed, the writings of his old rival, al-Ghazali, grew in stature. Even to this day, al-Ghazali remains an important figure in Islamic thought.

In the decades following Averroes's death, al-Andalus itself was waning in power. The great culture once centered in Córdoba disintegrated after many years of political turmoil. By the 1270s, Muslim Spain had been reduced to a small area around the city of

This fifteenth-century miniature depicts a Muslim funerary procession. In an act that surely would have pleased Averroes, his body of work was laid to rest next to the coffin containing his body. Averroes died in good standing with the caliph.

As the great cultural center of Córdoba came to an end, so did the Golden Age in Baghdad slowly die. This watercolor illustrates the conquest of Baghdad by Mongols. Although the Islamic world was changing, the works of its greatest minds would make it to Europe, where they would have new life.

Grenada. (By this time, the Abbasid caliphate based in Baghdad had also come to an end. The Abbasids, long in decline, lost all power in 1258, when their capital was overrun by invading tribes of Mongols from central Asia.)

But ironically, as al-Andalus was fading away, its influence over its European neighbors was beginning to grow. Leaving the dying city, scholars of al-Andalus began to scatter throughout Europe. With them, they brought new ideas and books, which eventually made their way to cities such as Paris, France; Bologna, Italy; and Oxford, England.

AVERROES'S INFLUENCE IN EUROPE

At the same time the Islamic world was turning away from philosophy, the Christian world was beginning to embrace it. The writings of the ancient Greeks had been largely unknown in western Europe for some six hundred years. Between the sixth and the twelfth centuries, European scholars had access to translations of only a few bits and pieces of Aristotle's and Plato's work. By the middle of the twelfth century, translations of some texts, most dealing with medicine and science, started reintroducing Europe to the intellectual legacy of the ancient world.

After Averroes's death, new translations of his works gave European scholars their first sustained taste of the ideas of Aristotle and Averroes's interpretations of them. Jewish scholars, translated some of them into Hebrew. These scholars were drawn to Averroes because he was held in great esteem by the Jewish philosopher Musa bin Maymun (known in the West as Moses Maimonides [1135–1204]), who himself was a well-regarded interpreter of Aristotle. A contemporary of Averroes, Maimonides was born in Córdoba, but fled al-Andalus after the Almohad rulers began forcing all non-Muslims to convert to Islam.

Maimonides was a contemporary of Averroes but was forced to flee Córdoba because he was a Sephardic Jew. Thanks to Maimonides's endorsement of Averroes, later Jewish scholars translated Averroes's work into Hebrew.

Maimonides eventually settled in Egypt, where Jews were granted religious freedom.

In the early thirteenth century, Averroes's work was also translated into Latin, the ancient Roman language well known to the learned. It was these translations that led the way to the rediscovery of Aristotle in western Europe. They were responsible for the full development of Scholasticism, a school of Christian thought that marked the golden age of philosophy in medieval Europe. Scholasticism sought a richer understanding of Christianity by examining its doctrines through reasoning and intellectual analysis.

During the thirteenth century, translations of Averroes's works became widely available at the universities that were springing up throughout Europe. Scholars were most interested in his commentaries on Aristotle. (His original works on philosophy and theology, such as *Incoherence of the Incoherence*, were far less widely read, probably because European Christians were not drawn to his musings on Islam.) In Europe, Averroes became so closely associated with Aristotle that he was often known merely as The Commentator.

Averroes's commentaries caused a stir among European intellectuals, in large part because of the challenge Greek philosophy seemed to pose to traditional religion. For more than 400 years, Islamic scholars had argued about whether philosophy and religion were compatible. Now, it was time for Christian thinkers to enter the debate.

The widespread interest in Averroes sparked a philosophical movement known as Averroism. Perhaps the most influential Averroist was Siger of Brabant (about 1240–1284). A professor at the University of Paris, he taught an interpretation of Aristotle that combined beliefs of Averroes and his fellow Islamic philosopher Avicenna.

A THREAT TO THE CATHOLIC CHURCH

Not surprisingly, Christian leaders saw Averroes as a threat. Often using arguments reminiscent of al-Ghazali's, they railed against his commentaries and the teaching of philosophy, claiming it was by its very nature incompatible with religious belief. One work challenging Averroes, written by theologian Albert the Great in 1256, was specifically commissioned by the head of the Catholic Church, Pope Alexander IV.

In the thirteenth century, the Catholic Church made several efforts to ban Averroes's work. In 1210, the study of his commentaries on Aristotle was prohibited in Paris. But as the city grew into the world's greatest intellectual center, more and more people ignored the ban. In 1277, Étienne Tempier, bishop of Paris, with the encouragement of Pope John XXI, launched another attack on Averroes's writings. He recorded a list of 219 ideas about God, the universe, and man's place in the universe. The Church objected to the ideas, many of which were specifically aimed at the Averroists. Among the condemned ideas were the eternity of the world, the impossibility of miracles, and the superior of philosophical truth over religious truth.

The Catholic Church also charged Siger of Brabant with heresy. Like other Averroists, he was accused of subscribing to the double-truth theory. This theory held that philosophy and religion provided such different ways of viewing the world that the same set of beliefs could be found true under one system and false under the other.

Averroes also came under attack by Thomas Aquinas (about 1224–1274), the leading Christian philosopher and theologian of the Middle Ages. While a student of Albert the Great at the University of Paris, Aquinas studied Aristotle and read the new Latin translations of Averroes's work. In 1270, he wrote *De Unitate Intellectus Contra Averroistas*, in which he criticized the philosophy of Averroes and his follower Siger of Brabant. Aquinas's greatest work, however,

Catholic bishop Albert the Great's scholarship on Aristotle's philosophies led him to study and publicly criticize the work of Averroes. Just as many in the Muslim world had railed against the study of philosophy, Albert believed that the discipline of philosophy could not coexist with religion.

was *Summa Thelogica*, in which he tried to reconcile Aristotle's work with Christian beliefs.

A QUESTION OF AUTHENTICITY

Aquinas's criticisms and the Catholic Church's condemnations slowed the spread of Averroism in Paris. Averroes's popularity was also diminished because Aquinas commissioned William of Moebeke to translate Aristotle's work directly into Latin. Many scholars came to favor these translations, and as a result, Averroes's paraphrases and interpretations of Aristotle lost some of their influence in Europe.

Nevertheless, Averroes continued to attract scholarly attention in Italy, particularly in the city of Padua. The most influential Averroist in Padua was John of Jandun (about 1286–1328). John of Jandun called Averroes "the most perfect and glorious physician, friend and fearless defender of the truth." Another Italian student of Averroes was the great poet Dante Alighieri (1265–1321). Averroes's philosophy greatly influenced his political treatise *De Monarchia*. After Dante's death, he was accused of Averroism, and Pope John XXII ordered the public burning of copies of *De Monarchia*.

Averroism continued well into the Renaissance. Lasting from the thirteenth to the sixteenth centuries, this period saw a renewed interest in the work of Greek and Roman writers. As the great commentator of Aristotle, Averroes remained an important figure for Renaissance scholars. But at the same time, the Renaissance also led to decreased interest in his work. More and more scholars learned Greek in order to have a more direct understanding of ancient texts. Because Averroes only knew Aristotle from Arabic translations, some students of philosophers came to question the authenticity of his interpretations.

A RESURGENCE

Interest in Averroes was revived during the nineteenth century, in large part because of the work of French philosopher Ernest Rénan. In 1852, Renan published *Averroes and the Averroists*, which chronicled Averroes's influence on the Western world. Some of Renan's claims, however, have been questioned by later scholars. He drew especially sharp criticism for his theory that the Averroists of the thirteenth century saw the philosophy of Averroes and Aristotle as being in complete opposition to Christian doctrine. Many scholars have also raised doubts about Renan's idea that these Averroists amounted to a kind of secret sect, who hoped to launch a stealth attack on

AVERROES IN THE ARTS

Reflecting his importance in Western culture, Averroes is referred to in two of the greatest literary works of the fourteenth century. In the prologue of *The Canterbury Tales*, the English poet Geoffrey Chaucer offers a list of medical authorities that includes Averroes. The reference makes clear that even 200 years after Averroes's death, his medical writings were still well known throughout Europe.

Averroes also makes an appearance in *The Divine Comedy* by Italian poet Dante Alighieri. In this poem, Dante takes a journey through hell, purgatory, and heaven. In hell, he encounters Saladin, the Egyptian warrior and political leader who led a Muslim army to capture Jerusalem from the hands of Christian crusaders in 1187. Around Saladin, Dante saw "his philosophic family" of great Greek and Islamic thinkers:

There, nearest him, and before the rest,
I saw Socrates and Plato...

I saw Dioscorides, the good taxonomist
Of plants, and I saw Orpheus,
Tully and Linus, and Seneca the moralist;

Euclid the geometer, and Ptolemy,
Hippocrates, Galen, Avicenna,
And Averroes who made the Great Commentary.

Raphael, another great Italian artist, also paid tribute to Averroes. In his fresco "School of Athens" (1510–1511), in the Stanza della Signatura in the Vatican Palace in Rome, Raphael depicted Plato and Aristotle in the center, surrounded by dozens of philosophers influenced by their teachings. At the far left, Averroes appeared, dressed in a green robe and white turban, intently looking over the shoulder of the Greek philosopher Pythagoras as he writes in a book. No image of Averroes made in his lifetime had survived, so Raphael's portrait is based solely on the painter's imagination.

In 1998, Averroes became an unlikely screen hero in *Destiny*, a film by famed Egyptian director Youssef Chahine. The romantic adventure is set in al-Andalus during the period when Averroes fell out of the caliph's favor. Chahine celebrates Averroes as a man of wisdom and conviction, even though his beliefs place him in harm's way.

Christianity. Nevertheless, Renan excited a renewed interest in Averroes among European scholars that continues until this day.

Renan's work also inspired a study of Averroes by Islamic scholar Farah Antun. In 1903, Antun wrote *Ibn Rushd and his Philosophy*, in which he attempted to link Averroes's rationalism with modern secularism. Antun was one of the leaders of Nahda, a movement that sought to combine Islamic and non-Islamic culture. Members of this movement embraced Averroes because, in their interpretation, his work exposed the differences between philosophy and religion. This served their goal of working to separate the church and the state in Islamic countries. Antun's book was highly controversial, but ultimately had little impact on Averroes's reputation in the East. Averroes remains an obscure figure in the Islamic world. Even today, the history of Islamic thought largely ignores Averroes's contributions.

In Western society, though, Averroes has left an indelible mark. He is still studied as one of the most comprehensive and intriguing interpreters of the work of Aristotle. But even more significantly, Averroes is seen as a crucial bridge between ancient and modern philosophy because of his role in introducing Europe to Greek thought.

TIMELINE

1126 Averroes (Ibn Rushd) is born in Córdoba in al-Andalus (Muslim Spain).

1146 The Almohad dynasty invades al-Andalus.

1153 Averroes travels to Marrakesh and begins to study astronomy.

1162 Averroes completes the medical treatise *Generalities in Medicine*.

1169 Averroes's friend Ibn Tufayl introduces him to the Almohad caliph, Abu Yaqub Yusuf, who commissions him to write commentaries on Aristotle. Averroes becomes a qadi (a religious judge) in Seville.

1170–1190 Averroes writes his major works on Aristotle.

1180 Averroes is appointed grand qadi of Córdoba.

1182 Averroes becomes the physician to the caliph.

1184 Averroes completes *Incoherence of the Incoherence*.

1191 Averroes completes his commentary on *Plato's Republic*.

1195 The Almohad authorities banish Averroes and burn his works.

1197 The caliph allows Averroes to return to Marrakesh and lifts the ban on his works.

1198 Averroes dies in Marrakesh, Morocco. His body is later returned to Córdoba for burial.

GLOSSARY

al-Andalus A portion of present-day Spain that was under Muslim rule from the eighth to the thirteenth centuries.

Averroism The thirteenth-century philosophical movement in Europe that was based on Averroes's commentaries on Aristotle.

caliph Successor to the prophet Muhammad. A ruler of the Muslim empire.

commentary An extended written interpretation or explanation.

deity God or goddess.

discourse Debate or authoritative commentary on a topic.

dynasty A succession of rulers from the same family.

emanationist Relating to a theory about the creation of the world, in which God was the starting point for a series of causes and effects that make up the structure of reality.

empire A group of territories or nations, often united by conquest and ruled by a single leader.

extant Surviving.

heresy An opinion that contradicts accepted religious beliefs.

hijra The Islamic prophet Muhammad's flight from Mecca to Medina in 622, which marks the beginning of the Muslim calendar.

infidel Person who does not believe in their own religion or who follows a different religion.

Islam A monotheistic religion based on the teachings of the prophet Muhammad and the words of the Koran.

Koran The sacred book of Islam, believed to be the word of God revealed to the prophet Muhammad.

mosque A Muslim house of worship.

Muslim A believer in Islam.

mystical Relating to a spiritual realm not discernible by the senses or by reason.

patron Individual who financially supports a person, cause, or organization.

philosophy The study of the nature of reality and principles underlying thinking and being.

qadi A Muslim judge who administers rulings based on the Koran.

Sharia The body of sacred Islamic law.

theology The study of God and religion.

treatise Formal discourse written on a subject.

FOR MORE INFORMATION

Arab Science and Technology Foundation
P.O. Box 2668
Sharjah, United Arab Emirates
+ 971 6 5584330
Website: http://www.astf.net/

The Arab Science and Technology Foundation is an independent, non-profit non-governmental organization that works regionally and internationally to encourage investment in Science and Technology.

Arab World and Islamic Resources (AWAIR)
P.O. Box 174
Abiquiu, NM 87510
(510) 704-0517
Website: http://www.awaironline.org

AWAIR's goal is to increase awareness and understanding of this world region and this world faith through educational outreach at the pre-collegiate level.

International Museum of Muslim Cultures
201 East Pascagoula Street
Jackson, Mississippi 39201
(601) 960-0440
Website: http://www.muslimmuseum.org
The International Museum of Muslim Cultures is dedicated to educating the American public about Islamic history and culture, the contribution of Muslims to the global community and the diversity of the Muslim community: past, present and future, including highlighting Metropolitan Jackson and the state's rich and diverse cultural and religious heritage.

Islamic Educational, Scientific, and Cultural Organization (ISESCO)
Avenue des F.A.R , Hay Ryad
PO Box 2275
+ 212 (0) 5 37 56 60 52 / 53
PC Code 10104 - Rabat - Kingdom of Morocco
Website: http://www.isesco.org.ma
(ISESCO) promotes cultural engagement and coordination in education, science, culture, and communication to highlight the achievements of Islamic culture and support socio-cultural development. The organization works closely with a number of international organizations on dialogue projects, especially the United Nations.

The Islamic Information Centre
460 Stapleton Road, Eastville
Bristol - BS5 6PA
United Kingdom
0117 902 0037
Website: http://www.islamicinformationcentre.co.uk

The Islamic Information Centre is a source of Islamic knowledge that offers a library of classical texts which cover topics such as Tasfeer, Aqidah, Fiqh, Tabaaqat (histories), Hadith studies, and educates the non-Muslim public on the religion of Islam.

Metropolitan Museum of Art
Islamic Art Division
1000 Fifth Avenue
New York, NY 10028
(212) 535-7710
Website: http://www.metmuseum.org/about-the-museum/museum-departments/curatorial-departments/islamic-art

The Metropolitan Museum of Art's collection of Islamic art features nearly twelve thousand objects ranging in date from the seventh to the nineteenth century. Comprising sacred and secular objects, the collection reveals the mutual influence of artistic practices such as calligraphy, and the exchange of motifs such as vegetal ornament (the arabesque) and geometric patterning in both realms.

Museum of Science and Technology in Islam
4700 King Abdullah University of Science & Technology
Thuwal 23955-6900
Kingdom of Saudi Arabia
Website: http://museum.kaust.edu.sa/
This museum is part of King Abdullah University of Science and Technology. It explores Islamic contributions to science and technology, including many from al-Kindi.

WEBSITES

Because of the changing nature of Internet links, Rosen Publishing has developed an online list of websites related to the subject of this book. This site is updated regularly. Please use this link to access this list:

http://www.rosenlinks.com/PSMI/averro

FOR FURTHER READING

Adamson, Peter and Peter E. Pormann. *The Philosophical Works of Al-Kindi*. Oxford, England: Oxford University Press, 2012.

Adamson, Peter. *In the Age of Averroes: Arabic Philosophy in the Sixth–Twelfth Century*. London: Warburg Institute School of Advanced Study, University of London, 2011.

Al-Khalili, Jim. *The House of Wisdom: How Arabic Science Saved Ancient Knowledge and Gave Us the Renaissance*. New York: Penguin Press, 2011.

Al-Khalili, Jim. *Pathfinders: The Golden Age of Arabic Science*. London: Penguin, 2012.

Barber, Nicola. *Medieval Medicine*. Chicago, IL: Raintree, 2013.

Belting, Hans. *Florence and Baghdad: Renaissance Art and Arab Science*. Cambridge, MA: Belknap Press of Harvard University Press, 2011.

Bobrick, Benson. *The Caliph's Splendor: Islam and the West in the Golden Age of Baghdad*. New York: Simon & Schuster, 2012.

Collins, Roger. *Caliphs and Kings: Spain, 796-1031*. Malden, MA: Wiley-Blackwell, 2012.

Freely, John. *Light from the East: How the Science of Medieval Islam Helped to Shape the Western World*. New York: Palgrave Macmillan, 2011.

Fuess, Albrecht and Jan-Peter Hartung. *Court Cultures in the Muslim World: Seventh to Nineteenth Centuries*. New York, NY: Routledge, 2011.

Heschel, Abraham Joshua. *Maimonides*. New York, NY: Fall River Press, 2012.

Lapidus, Ira M. *A History of Islamic Societies*. New York: Cambridge University Press, 2014.

Nardo, Don. *The Birth of Islam*. Greensboro, NC: Morgan Reynolds Publishing, 2012.

Resnick, Irven M. *A Companion to Albert the Great: Theology, Philosophy, and the Science*. Leiden: Brill, 2013.

Romanek, Trudee. *Science, Medicine, and Math in the Early Islamic World*. New York: Crabtree Publishing Company, 2012.

Roscoe, Kelly and Mick Isle. *Aristotle: The Father of Logic*. New York: Rosen Publishing, 2016.

Ruthven, Malise. *Islam: A Very Short Introduction*. New York: Oxford University Press, 2012.

Saliba, George. *Islamic Science and the Making of the European Renaissance*. Cambridge, MA: MIT Press, 2011.

Scherer, Lauri S. *Islam*. Detroit, MI: Greenhaven Press, 2012.

Urvoy, Dominique. *Ibn Rushd* (Averroes). New York: Routledge, 2015.

BIBLIOGRAPHY

Arnaldez, Roger. *Averroes: A Rationalist in Islam*. Translated by David Streight. Notre Dame, IN: University of Notre Dame Press, 2000.

Averroes. *Faith and Reason in Islam*. Translated by Ibrahim Najjar. Oxford, UK: Oneworld Publications, 2001.

Esposito, John L., ed. *The Oxford History of Islam*. New York, NY: Oxford University Press, 1999.

Fakhry, Majid. *A Short Introduction to Islamic Philosophy*, Theology, and Mysticism. Oxford, UK: Oneworld Publications, 1997.

Fakhry, Majid. *Averroes: His Life, Works and Influence*. Oxford, UK: Oneworld Publications, 2001.

Hayes, John R., ed. *The Genius of Arab Civilization*. 3rd ed. New York, NY: New York University Press, 1992.

Leaman, Oliver. *A Brief Introduction to Islamic Philosophy*. Cambridge, UK: Polity Press, 1999.

Leaman, Oliver. *Averroes and His Philosophy*. Richmond, UK: Curzon, 1998.

Menocal, María Rosa. *The Ornament of the World*. Boston, MA: Little, Brown and Company, 2002.

Stone, Caroline. "Doctor, Philosopher, Renaissance Man." *Saudi Aramco World*, Vol. 54, No. 3, May/June 2003, pp. 8–15.

INDEX

G

H

I

J

K

L

M

ABOUT THE AUTHORS

Bridget Lim has taught history and religion at the high school level. Currently, she is pursuing a PhD in Islamic Studies.

Liz Sonneborn is a writer, living in Brooklyn, New York. A graduate of Swarthmore College, she has written more than fifty books for children and adults. Specializing in American and world history, she has a particular interest in the cultures and philosophy of the ancient world.

PHOTO CREDITS

Cover De Agostini Picture Library/Getty Images; cover (background), pp. 3, 26, 27, 38, 52, 77, 94, 95 gfxmart/Shutterstock.com; p. 5 Iqbal Khatri/Moment/Getty Images; pp. 6-7 kickimages/E/Getty Images; pp. 7 (inset), 66-67, 84-85 Pictures from History/Bridgeman Images; p. 13 Leemage/Universal Images Group/Getty Images; pp. 18-19 Print Collector/Hulton Archive/Getty Images; pp. 22-23 George Munday/age fotostock/SuperStock; p. 27 Artur Bogacki/Shutterstock.com; pp. 28-29 Falconaumanni/Wikimedia/File:Taifas2.gif/CC BY-SA 3.0; pp. 32-33 LOOK-foto/SuperStock; p. 35 Bibliotheque de la Faculte de Medecine, Paris, France/Archives Charmet/Bridgeman Images; p. 36 Courtesy Jeff Miller; p. 40 IgorGolovniov/Shutterstock.com; p. 42 Nikita Maykov/Shutterstock.com; pp. 50-51 Private Collection/Photo © Tarker/Bridgeman Images; p. 55 © histopics/ullstein bild/The Image Works; p. 57 © Art Directors & TRIP/Alamy Stock Photo; p. 58 DEA/G. Dagli Orti/DeAgostini/Getty Images; pp. 68-69 Museo Correr, Venice, Italy/Bridgeman Images; p. 70 Science Source, colorization by Meredith Carlson; p. 75 The National Library of Medicine; pp. 80-81 Sheila Terry/Science Source; p. 83 De Agostini Picture Library/Bridgeman Images; p. 87 Georgios Kollidas/Shutterstock.com; p. 91 Apic//Hulton Archive/Getty Images; p. 96 Scala/Art Resource, NY; additional cover and interior background patterns and textures javarman/Shutterstock.com, Dragana Jokmanovic/Shutterstock.com; back cover pattern MaryMo/Shutterstock.com

Designer: Michael Moy; Editor: Christine Poolos;
Photo Researcher: Nicole DiMella